WE DRIVE

Oversize Load Trucks

Ruby Tuesday Books

Alix Wood

Published in 2026 by Ruby Tuesday Books Ltd.

Editors: Ruth Owen & Mark J. Sachner
Design & Production: Alix Wood

Photo credits:
Alamy: 15B (Taina Sohlman), 16T (Robert McGouey/Industry), 16B (Adwo), 17T (Peter Titmuss), 17B (Jim West), 19B (Rob Gray), 20 (Everett Collection Inc), 21 (JMF News); Shutterstock: Cover (Shooting it), 1 (Nuad Contributor), 3 (Pru Sanderson), 4 (Gilles Paire), 5 (Uwe Aranas), 6 (thelamephotographer), 7T (knelson20), 7B (fotografiko eugen), 8T (Vladimir Konstantinov), 8B (Tong__stocker), 9T (sky-lord), 9B (F Armstrong Photography), 10T (Antoni M Lubek), 11T (3D-Horse), 11B (vladdon), 12 (Thongchai.S), 13 (amophoto__au), 14B (vladdon), 15T (Andriy Blokhin), 18–19 (Rigucci), 22T (aappp), 22C (Joseph Sohm), 22B (Oleksiy Mark), 23T (Around the World), 23C (aappp), 23B (Vitpho); Alix Wood: 10B.

Library of Congress Control Number: 2024949068

Print (Hardback) ISBN 978-1-78856-531-8
Print (Paperback) ISBN 978-1-78856-532-5
ePub ISBN 978-1-78856- 533-2

Published in Minneapolis, MN
Printed in the United States

www.rubytuesdaybooks.com

Contents

How Do Trucks Deliver Giant Loads?

Truck drivers deliver all kinds of **cargo** every day.

Sometimes they must haul an oversize **load**—such as a house!

An oversize load can be very wide, extra long, super tall, or mega heavy.

It takes lots of skill to transport an oversize load.

Before a driver delivers an oversize load, they must figure out what **route** to take.

They check a map to look for narrow roads and tight turns.

They check for low or weak bridges and low overhead wires.

The truck driver may also check the route for dangers by driving it in a car.

Low overhead wires

A driver checks the truck's tires before loading the cargo.

The tires must have plenty of air to carry a giant load.

Sometimes, oversize cargo is loaded onto a truck by crane.

The driver uses thick chains to make sure the load is secure and won't fall off.

Some **trailers** can stretch to help carry long loads!

The driver unlocks a pin and pulls the trailer to make it longer.

Some trailers can drop down to the ground to make them easier to load.

The trailer is lower than the wheels.

A low trailer also helps the driver fit a tall load under low bridges.

Sometimes a huge oversize load is moved by a giant trailer called an SPMT.

An oil rig on an SPMT

Wheels

An SPMT is made by joining together lots of trailer-like sections with wheels.

The driver uses a remote control to steer an SPMT and make it move or stop.

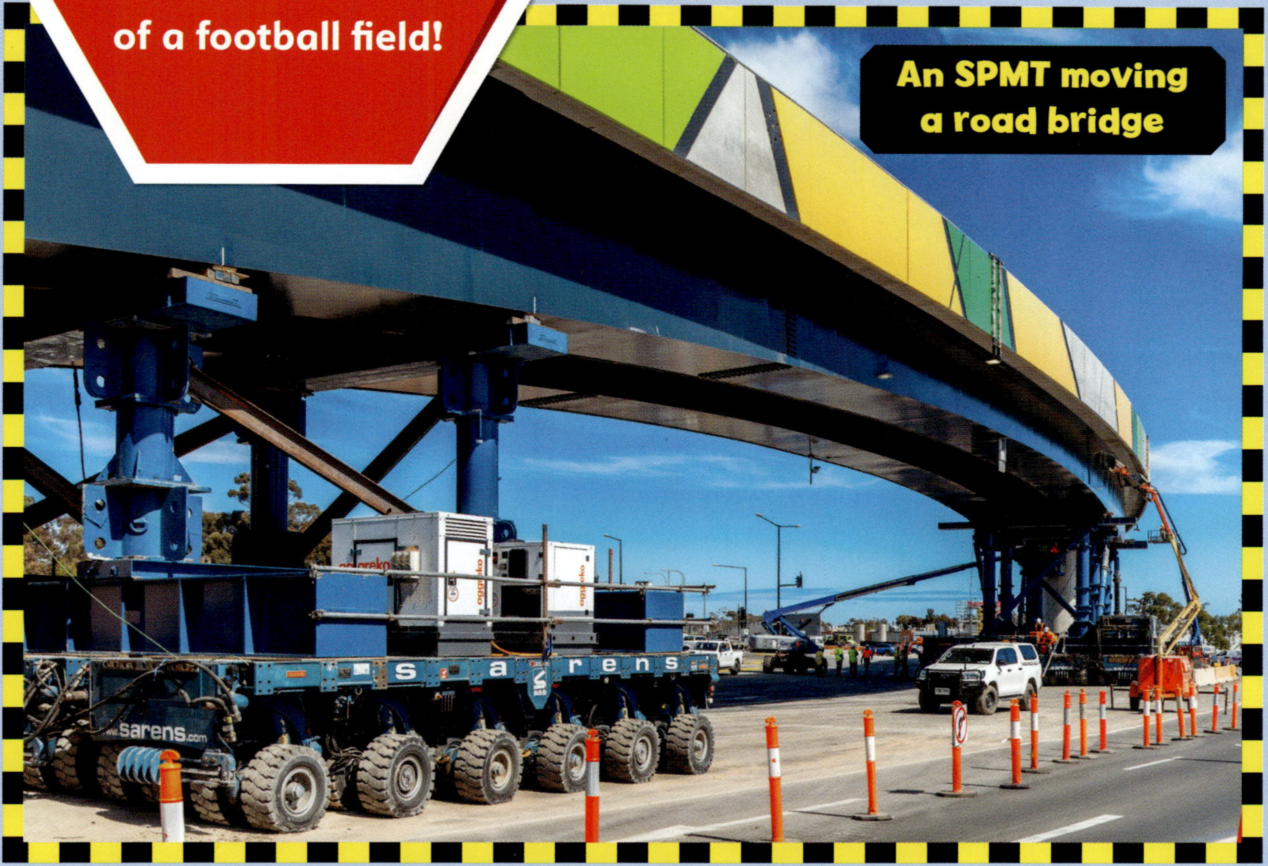

SPMT stands for Self-Propelled Modular Transporter. It can be the size of a football field!

An SPMT moving a road bridge

Each wheel can be turned, lifted, or lowered into a different position from the wheels around it.

Oversize load drivers must show other vehicles that they are carrying an extra wide or long load.

Oversize loads have warning signs on the front, back, and sides of the truck.

Warning signs

Drivers put red or orange flags on the load.

Flags

OVERSIZE LOAD

Oversize load trucks may have flashing lights to tell other drivers—giant load coming through!

An oversize load truck may have escort vehicles.

The escort might drive in front of the truck to warn drivers coming the other way.

This car has pulled over to let the truck pass.

An escort vehicle may drive behind or next to the truck.

This warns cars not to pass, or to pass with care.

Sometimes a very wide or long load may have a police escort.

A police car blocks a road so an oversize load can make a turn.

A truck must have a very long trailer to move a wind turbine blade.
Cab
Wheels
Escort vehicle
Trailer
Wheels
A wind turbine blade can be as long as seven school buses parked end to end!

Sometimes a blade is too long to travel through a small town.

A machine on the truck lifts the blade up.

A driver must drive an oversize load very slowly and very carefully.

In 2012, a giant rock, which was part of an artwork, was moved in California.

The truck carrying the rock moved so slowly, it had to travel at night to keep from holding up daytime traffic.

In 2013, a giant part of an electricity plant, called a transformer, was moved in the United Kingdom.

The truck crawled along at 4 miles (6.5 km) per hour.

Every day, oversize load drivers are busy delivering HUGE loads!

Glossary

cargo
Goods that are collected and delivered by trucks, trains, planes, or ships.

load
The objects being carried by a truck. Also the word for putting goods onto a truck.

route
The roads taken to get from one place to another.